Thos L. Johnson

A Careful Study of the Missionary Field in Africa

Thos L. Johnson

A Careful Study of the Missionary Field in Africa

ISBN/EAN: 9783743419117

Manufactured in Europe, USA, Canada, Australia, Japa

Cover: Foto ©Lupo / pixelio.de

Manufactured and distributed by brebook publishing software
(www.brebook.com)

Thos L. Johnson

A Careful Study of the Missionary Field in Africa

"GIVE A THOUGHT TO AFRICA."

A CAREFUL

STUDY OF THE MISSIONARY FIELD

IN

AFRICA.

BY

REV. THOS. L. JOHNSON,

A Returned Missionary.

CHICAGO:

THE CONSERVATOR PRINT, 162 AND 164 SOUTH CLARK STREET.

1881.

INTRODUCTORY.

OFFICE OF CORRESPONDING SECRETARY OF THE WOOD
RIVER BAPTIST ASSOCIATION OF ILLINOIS,
12 GANO ST., CHICAGO, ILL.

The interest that is being awakened in Evangelical Christian Missions in Africa, is an occasion of thanksgiving, and renewed diligence, perseverance and faith, on the part of those who have long prayed and labored for the spread of the gospel in that land of grossest heathenism and spiritual darkness. Other uncivilized and heathen countries may, perhaps, present fewer and less destructive barriers to the introduction and spread of the gospel, but none can have any higher claims, or present a more importunate plea to Christian people in all lands, and of all races, to furnish them with "the bread of life," than

PERISHING MILLIONS IN AFRICA.

But to her own children and their descendents, her appeals "to come over and help us," should awaken a deeper interest, and be the inspiration of a more abiding enthusiasm than has as yet been manifested. The Christian religion has lifted other races and other lands from degradation and superstition into the highest civilization and advancement. It can and will do the same for Africa. And of whom can she ask this boon for her sons and daughters at home, with more force, than of her sons and daughters in other lands, and especially in America, so far as they have the means and ability to give it to them?

THE CHRISTIAN CIVILIZATION OF AFRICA

is the one thing needed to estop the prejudgment that hangs over the heads of her descendents in every other land, and represses them in every avenue of endeavor. Its accomplishment will wipe out the reproaches wherewith they are now reproached.

I have known the author of this little pamphlet for many years as an earnest worker for the evangelization of his race, both in America and in Africa. He has encountered and overcome difficulties in the way of his advancement and the prosecution of his much-loved work, to which a less determined and persevering mind would have succumbed.

THE WOOD RIVER BAPTIST ASSOCIATION, OF ILLINOIS,

has appointed him to superintend the missionary work within her bounds, with the especial view to the awakening of interest in African missionary work in the churches. I hereby endorse him, and commend him to the churches and the benevolence of christians everywhere.

REV. R. DeBAPTISTE,
Cor. Sec'y.

PREFACE.

The christian world is growing daily more interested in the evangelization of heathen lands. This may not be apparent to the casual observer, but the diligent enquirer after truth will find, to his great joy, that spiritual welfare of heathen nations is becoming a matter of prayerful anxiety among all classes of true christians.

After being abroad four years, the writer returned home in August, 1880. The following September I met the Wood River Baptist Association at Jacksonville, Ill. After laying before that body the claims of Africa, I was appointed superintendent of domestic and foreign missionary work. I at once commenced to travel from place to place, trying to awaken a deeper interest among colored people for African mission work, and lecturing to raise means to send missionaries to Africa.

On my journey I met with many who wanted a copy of my lecture. Often after the lecture was over friends would ask me questions which had not been mentioned in my discourse. This suggested the idea that a small pamphlet, cheap enough to be in the reach of all, giving a few facts of Africa's former condition as collected from history, her present deplorable condition, the great success of missionary work on the west coast and my personal experience, would not only meet this demand, but might awaken a deeper interest for African mission work.

I know that Africa has many wise and noble advocates. This little pamphlet is only a feeble effort to help on the great work. Every nail driven into the building makes it that much strouger. In sending forth this little work my prayer is, that the information given may make many friends for Africa, and redound to the glory of God.

My dear friends, please "give a thought to Africa." God seems now to be saying to the christian world, "I have set before thee an open door" in Africa, " go, and lo, I am with you," to deliver that long oppressed race from darkness, degradation and shame. It is our indispensable duty as christians, to do all we can to send the gospel to these benighted people.

Yours for the evangelization of Africa,

THOS. L. JOHNSON,

CHICAGO, ILL.

April 20th, 1881.

GIVE A THOUGHT TO AFRICA.

Give a thought to Africa!
  'Neath the burning sun
There are hosts of weary hearts
  Waiting to be won:
Many idols have they made,
  But, from swamp and sod
There are voices crying now
  For the living God.

Chorus—

    Tell the love of Jesus
      By her hills and waters;
    God bless Africa,
      And her sons and daughters.

Breathe a prayer for Africa!
  God the Father's love
Can reach down and bless the tribes
  From His Heaven above.
Swarthy lips when moved by grace
  Ever sweetly sing;
Pray that Afric hearts be made
  Loyal to our King.

    Tell the love of Jesus, &c.

Give support to Africa!
  Has not English gold
Been the gain of tears and blood
  When the slaves were sold?
Let us send the gospel back,
  Since, for all their need,
Those whom Jesus Christ makes free
  Shall be free indeed.

Tell the love of Jesus, &c.

Give your love to Africa!
  They are brothers all,
Who by sin and slavery
  Long were held in thrall.
Let the white man love the black,
  And, when time is past,
In "Our Father's house" above
  May all meet at last.

Tell the love of Jesus, &c.

Written by Miss Marianne Farningham, Northampton, England, for
Rev. Thos. L. Johnson.

AN UNKNOWN LAND.

Of no country in the world has so little hith-
erto been known as of Africa. Recent discoveries
in Africa, however, mark the present as an interesting crisis in her history. No country in
the world has stronger claims upon christendom
than Africa, which has for ages been the crippled
limb of humanity. From century to century
she has remained almost in sight of civilized
nations, enriching them with her ivory, drugs,
woods, and metals, receiving in exchange a few
insignificant beads, and rum, which is a curse to
the country.

All these years she has remained uncivilized,
and, for the most part, unknown. Up to the
present day, there are thousands of people who
know more about almost every part of the world
than of Africa. From generation to generation
it has lain a blank on the map of nations. For
hundreds of years the names of a few places
around the coasts have been known, but not until the discoveries of Burton, Schweinfurth,
Speak, Grant, Dr. Livingstone, whose name will
live as long as Africa exists, and Cameron,
Stanley and many others, did the world begin

to know anything about the vast interior, with
its neglected, perishing millions of heathen,
knowing nothing of the one true God.

But the dawn of a brighter day grows on
apace. Thank God, a door effectual has been
opened to the great interior, and Christians of
every name and nation are at work sending the
everlasting gospel to that long-neglected continent. Our God, who is the God of the oppressed, is about to reclaim an injured race.
Africa is said to contain one-fourth part of the
entire land area of the globe. It is five thousand
miles in length from north to south, and four
thousand six hundred miles in breadth from east
to west. Bounded on the north by the Mediterranean Sea, separating it from Europe ; on the
east by the Indian Ocean, the Red Sea and
Asia, and on the west by the Atlantic Ocean,
which separates it from the American coast. It
is estimated to have a population of largely
over two hundred millions of people.

By giving a thought to Africa, we cannot fail
to be struck with the magnitude and importance
of this vast continent. We, as Christians, enjoying the blessed privileges of the gospel,

> " Who were not born as thousands are,
>   Where God was never known ;
> And taught to pray a useless prayer,
>   To blocks of wood and stone,"

should know more about this vast continent, and

its neglected, perishing millions of heathen. We should know more about the condition of the many tribes inhabiting this long-neglected continent, which has for ages presented nothing but desolation, ruin and misery. Oh, think of it! For centuries the blessed gospel has been preached, and made most wonderful progress, while millions in Africa have lived and died, having never heard of the one true God, or of our blessed Jesus.

Age after age they have been alllowed to sit in darkness and the shadow of Death ; no one to bring to them the message of eternal life.

STORY OF NATIVE CONVERTS.

While in England, I attended a missionary meeting with the late Rev. Alfred Sakes, who spent thirty years in Africa. He told a very

TOUCHING STORY OF A NATIVE CONVERT.

He said to the missionary : "There is one thing I want to ask, Where is my father ? He died ; he never heard of Jesus ; your people have heard of Jesus for ages. How is it that you white people could send here for slaves, and not send us word about Jesus ?" Dr. Livingstone says, when he told a South African Chief of the great white throne and Him who shall sit on it, from whose face the heaven and earth shall flee away, he said, "You startle me, these words make all my bones to shake ; I have no more strength in me. My forefathers were liv-

ing at the time yours were, and how is it that
they did not send them word about these terrible
things sooner ?"

For ages, the mothers and fathers by millions
have been passing from time into eternity, knowing nothing of the great plan of salvation, and
that too almost in sight of civilization. No part
of the world has stronger claim upon the Chris-
tion Church to-day, than long-oppressed, long-
neglected Africa.

While attending the C. A. B. M. convention
in Baltimore, Md., October, 1880, a gentleman
asked me, " Why is it that Africa has been in
the condition she is, for so many years ?" This
is a question which no doubt hundreds have
asked. It is a question I have often asked myself in years past. Why is it, that while
other nations have risen and fallen, and risen
again, and gone on successfully, Africa, the land
of my fathers, has been going down, down,
from bad to worse, from century to century?
Before I attempt to give what seems to me, at
least, the reason why she has thus remained for
the past four or five centuries, we will ask another question : Has Africa always been in this
condition ?

AFRICA OF THE ANCIENTS.

The only knowledge we have of any country, nation or people, is what we gather from history. The historian tells us that Africa, of which so little is now known, not only flourished at one period of the world, but that she was the cradle of the arts and sciences; that when Greece was yet young, and Rome unknown, before Abraham was, or the Jewish commonwealth had a name, Africa could boast of old and. civilized kingdoms.* Africa once had her churches, her colleges, her repositories of the sciences and learning, her Cyprians and Bishops of apostolic renown, and her noble army of martyrs.† Africa, the land of my fathers, has indeed, been a highly-favored country. It was in Africa that Moses, the most extraordinary man that lived in the early ages, was born and educated. ·

When all Europe and Western Asia lay sunk in deep darkness, there was light in Africa. And again, when in the "Dark Ages," the light of Greece and Rome had suffered an eclipse, and darkness once more settled down over Europe, there was light in Africa.

---

*Negro problem solved.
†Moffatt's Southern Africa.

The first permanent advance made by the world in literature, and for the perpetuation of science, was the invention of an alphabet; this we owe to Egypt. The alphabet was a result of Egyptian hieroglyphics. Cadmus is said to have brought into Greece sixteen letters of the alphabet 1519 years before Christ. Learning, like the alphabet, traveled from Africa into Europe through the Phœnicians, another branch of the family of Ham. The progress made by certain African states in the sciences of civil government indicates the advanced condition of these states.

Systems of government imply the existence of wise statesmen, and institutions of learning and civil polity. These are never found except in an advanced state of civilization.

CARTHAGE BEFORE ITS FALL.

Carthage was a republic and enjoyed perhaps the most perfect system of civil polity which has fallen to the lot of any nation before Great Britain. Her government was far in advance of any other ancient government save the Jewish.

She took the lead in all which exalts human nature, and confers the highest blessings on society. Her provinces were opulent and enlightened, including nearly the whole of North and West Africa and the islands of the Mediterranean. She could boast of renowned sages and learned fathers of the church.*

---

*Negro problem solved. .

"Carthage became one of the greatest commercial cities in the world; the number of the inhabitants before its destruction amounted to 700,000."*

Rev. H. Read, speaking of the African races as being pioneers and the first cultivators of the arts and sciences, says : " We would therefore seem to hazard nothing in the conclusion that commerce and the arts, science and learning, civilization and human improvement in general, were first identified with and developed through a race that has now for long ages been associated only with degradation and barbarous ignorance." Dr. Smythe says : "We may, therefore, as philosophical inquirers seeking after truth, admit the full force of any facts which may encourage the belief that there was a time when the black race of men were the pioneers, or at least the equals of any other races in all the arts and acquirements of man's primitive civilization." Africa has indeed presented some noble specimens of manhood, men who were profound thinkers and acute reasoners, men who were advocates of truth and equity, men who were able writers and zealous defenders of the christian religion.

A FEW GREAT MEN.

Cyprian, who lived in the third century, was an African, born in Carthage. He became one

*Chambers' Encyclopædia.

of the fathers of the church in Africa; in conse-
quence of his profound piety he was made bishop
of the church.   History tells us that he was both
a learned and eloquent divine.   His writings
were very extensive.   Athanasius was born in
Alexandria   He distinguished himself when
quite a youth, on account of persecutions.   He
became an exile in the Egyptian desert, where
he wrote several works to confirm orthodox
christians in their faith.   From this time twenty
years of his life were spent in exile, or what was
equivalent to it.   He was the leading ecclesiastic
in the most trying period of the history of the
early christian church.   His ability, his judi-
ciousness and wisdom, his fearlessness in the
storms of opposition, his activity and patience,
all mark him out as an ornament of the age as
well as the most influential public character in
matters of Religion.[*]

ST.   AUGUSTINE

was born in the year of 354 at Tagaste, a town
in Numidia, North Africa.   At sixteen he went
to Carthage to complete his education.   He was
a man of rare learning and very industrious; it
was recorded that he was the author of two hundred and thirty separate treatises on theological
subjects.   In the year of 397 appeared his con-
fession in thirteen books.   It is a deep, earnest
and sacred autobiography of one of the greatest

*Chamber's Encyclopædia.

intellects the world has seen. Passages of it have no parallel except in the psalms of David. His work is one of the most profound and lasting monuments of human genius. No mind has exerted greater influence on the church than that of St. Augustine.*

ARNOBIUS,

an African, became a christian in the third century. He wrote several books in which he defended the christian religion. Origen, Clement, and many others we have not the space in this little book to mention, were as able teachers and advocates of the christian religion, as are to be found in the history of any other nation.

Not only has Africa been the fatherland and home of the scholar, the philosopher, statesman, architect and learned divines. It was in Africa our blessed Jesus sought refuge, and when on His way up the hill of Calvary He chose that an African should help Him bear His cross. From what we gather from the historian, Africa of the Ancients was not one whit behind any other country on the globe.

---

*Chambers' Encyclopædia.

Native Africans have shown themselves masters in every station in life ; but the light which shone so beautifully many centuries ago in Africa, has long since given place to great darkness. What Africa has once been, religious training can make her again, and when the christian family does her duty to Africa, her sons will not be found wanting when called upon in the future to take part in the great events yet to transpire.

Now, then, to the question. How Africa (in such an advanced state of civilization) lost her position, degenerated and became enveloped in darkness, we cannot tell. "Whether it lies in the early and utter destruction of the primitive church of North Africa by the Saracenic conquests, completely exterminating the faith of Christ in those regions, or whether in the universal and long-continued apostasy of the church of the middle ages," we cannot tell. But why has she continued thus (for four or five centuries) in darkness and the shadow of death, while other nations have been making such progress in literature, the arts, sciences and religion. Of all the long and dark catalogue of crime in Africa, the land of my fathers, we have only space to mention one gigantic evil, which we claim to be the cause of her condition for the past four or five centuries.

THE CURSE OF SLAVERY.

Slavery will degrade any nation upon the face of God's earth. It can be shown that in all ages and climes slavéry and oppression has resulted in ignorance, degradation, carnage and death.

From the able work of the Rev. Hollis Read, who has given to the world a most interesting account of African history, I have collected the following : " Of all the nations that have cursed Africa, the Portuguese have been the direst curse. These people visited Africa during the early part of the fourteenth century, seized and made slaves of the natives. In the course of time they controlled the west coast of Africa.

OTHER CAUSES OF DEGRADATION.

There is not a blacker page in history than that which records the atrocities of the Portuguese in Africa. One writer says the Portuguese were men of the basest behavior, cruel and corrupt above all men.

Then Africa became a place of banishment for criminals convicted of various outrages ; a place where adventurers (who hated the restraint of the law) sought freedom. The natives themselves, in their lamentable condition, detested

the shameless atrocities of their visitors. Then
came also the Dutch, introducing rum and other
vices.

Herds of pirates next infested the coast.
They spread themselves over the whole coast,
and there commenced and continued unheard of
cruelties. Perfectly versed in all the vices of
civilization, when not at sea, they committed the
most remorseless depredations on shore.

Following these came the Jesuits, who only
perpetuated what the Portuguese had commenced.
Their religion (says an officer who was on the
coast) was a religion of money and blood ; it was
without truth, without a Sabbath, and without
mercy. It brought with it no truth-telling bible,
no sacred rest.

HOW SLAVES WERE CAPTURED.

All of these classes had a hand in the slave trade. The cruelties of the capture are, in my opinion, what has broken the people up into so many clans and petty tribes. A trader contracts with some king for from one to five hundred slaves. He promises to assist the king in the capture. At night when all is quiet, this king, assisted by the trader and his men, surprises the inhabitants of some peaceful town or city. The work of plunder, murder and bloodshed is commenced. Houses are at once set on fire. All the old men and women and young children are murdered, while the able-bodied young men and women are taken and made slaves. It is recorded that on these occasions from 20,000 to 60,000 became victims to slaughter. Many would make their escape to the mountains and caves, where they were followed. If they could not be induced to come out, fires were built at the entrance, and they either suffocated or compelled to come out. One writer says: "I should think that in addition to the 7,000 or 8,000 taken captives, at least 15,000 were killed in defense or suffocation at the time of being taken. This has been carried on from age to age, district after district being broken up."

Speaking of the moral desolation of Africa by this trade, a writer says : "All moral virtue has been extinguished in the people, their industry annihilated by this one ruinous curse. This trade, carried on for years, has destroyed all society, all confidence. Large cities having been burnt and districts broken up, the people live in clans in different parts of the country, each man suspicious of his neighbor. It has no doubt been the principal cause of war for hundreds of years."

Governor Ashman speaks of large sections of country once fertile and under a high state of cultivation, but since completely depopulated and reduced to a desert by the slave trade.

For hundreds of years Africa has been brought in contact with the most outrageous and cruel class of men on the face of the earth. Can you wonder at the condition of Africa after having such tutors and such training? The question should not be, Why has Africa remained in this condition, but the wonder should be that there is a single redeeming feature left; that its people are not totally corrupt and sunk into the depths of human corruption. Deep, deep, indeed, has Africa's sons drank the dregs of human bitterness. Perhaps no nation has been compelled to pass through such a school, under such tutors, as the people of Africa.

A LABOR OF LOVE.

Knowing something of the sufferings of my fatherland, I had an intense desire to go to Africa. This was soon after my conversion in 1857. I felt anxious to go and preach the gospel. Being a slave, no door was opened for me to prepare myself for this great work. For many years, therefore, it was my secret desire to go to Africa and preach the gospel to my own, long-benighted people. Long before I entered the ministry I often thought of it.

After I was ordained in Olivet Baptist church, Chicago, Ill., April 15th, 1869, I was called to take charge of a church in Denver, Colorado, where I remained for three years. The desire to go to Africa never left me. I resigned and returned to Chicago with the intention of preparing myself for the African mission work. Friends persuaded me not to go. Even my beloved father in the gospel, Rev. R. DeBaptiste, persuaded me to remain in the State of Illinois, which I did for four years and five months.

Having served over 28 years as a slave in Virginia, deprived of the advantages of an education, friends in England sent for me to come to that country to pursue a course of study before

going to Africa.   Mr. and Mrs. E. S. Smith had
interceded for me after their return home to
England.

After a two years' course at Rev. C. H. Spurgeon's College in London, I was sent out by the
Baptist Missionary Society of Great Britain as a
missionary to Africa.   November 6th, 1878,
Rev. C. H. Richardson and his wife, my wife
and myself bade farewell to the dear, kind friends
in London.   We arrived in Manchester in the
afternoon, spent the night with our friends, Mr. ·
E. S. Smith's family, who were the means of
our being in England.   On Saturday afternoon,
Nov. 9th, at 3:30, we sailed from Liverpool on
the *S. S. Kinsembo.*

LIFE IN AFRICA.

November 16th we came in sight of the island of Poto Santo. On awaking from sleep the next morning we found ourselves anchored at Funchal, the capitol of the island of Maderia, a beautiful little town with a population of about 30,-000. After stopping at Grand Canaria and Teneriffe, on the evening of Nov. 22d we came in sight of Cape Verde on the west coast of Africa, where there is a large French colony. As soon as I caught sight of the peak, nearly 30 miles off, I went into my stateroom for my telescope. For years my prayer had been that I might see Africa, the land of my fathers, and now my prayer was answered.

"Delight thyself also in the Lord; and He shall give thee the desires of thine heart. Commit thy way unto the Lord; trust also in Him; and He shall bring it to pass."—Psalms, 37, 45.

I can never describe my feelings of joy. I could not leave my stateroom without falling upon my knees and thanking my Heavenly Father for permitting me to see the land of poor, suffering Africa. I was so delighted that I was near the coast of Africa, the land for which I had prayed and of which I had dreamed, I could sleep but a few hours. On the morning of the 23d I was up at 4 o'clock to get another look at the land of my fathers. Soon I was informed that we had entered

THE MOUTH OF THE GAMBIA RIVER.

As we proceeded up the river I heard that a pilot was expected to meet us. Having been 14 days on the steamer, we were all anxious once more to get on land. Soon we saw a small boat. "There's the pilot, there's the pilot," cried out first one and then another. The little boat was quickly by the side of the steamer. The pilot came on board. He was a native. As soon as I could I had an interview with him. I found him to be a christian and quite an intelligent man. His name was Wm. Halfner.

ON DRY LAND.

Soon we found ourselves anchored at the beautiful little town of Bathurst on the Gambia river. This settlement was formed for the suppression of the slave trade and the encouragement of legitimate commerce. It is about 10 miles from the mouth of the river. It contains quite a number of fine dwelling-houses. Here we put our feet on African soil for the first time.

The chief stores of European merchants front the river. I was quite surprised to find such fine stone buildings, a fine Government house and barracks and hospital on a line fronting the river.

Mr. Walcott, a colored lawyer, who had been educated in England, invited us to his house, as also did Mr. Brown, American Consul.

We had quite a nice time going around the town, meeting with different native gentlemen holding office under the English Government. The Harbor Master, Postmaster, City Clerk, Queen's Consul and the Custom House officers were all native black men. Here we met native merchants, ship builders, men in almost every capacity of business, educated either in England or Sierra Leone.

There were also two fine churches and a thriv-day school, which made my heart glad.

Here we had the first opportunity of seeing the tall Mandingoes, Joloffs and natives of other tribes in their native dress. In the back part of the town we saw many native huts formed of bamboo, thatched with long grass.

The Gambia river is a magnificent stream, and is said to be navigable for vessels to a distance of nearly 400 miles. What is better still, here the messengers of life have met with great success in proclaiming the everlasting gospel. On the morning of Nov. 27th we entered the harbor of Free Town.

LIFE IN SIERRA LEONE.

The first British settlement formed on the west coast of Africa for the suppression of the slave trade and the encouragement of legitimate commerce was Sierra Leone. Freetown is the capital, and is indeed a beautiful place. It is situated on the south side of the river. The first view we got of this beautiful town was perfectly grand. The land in the neighborhood inclines gradually upwards into hills, covered everywhere with vegetation, presenting a most picturesque scene. Many of the buildings are of a very substantial character.

Almost every house has its nice large yard and garden, in which the banana, orange, cocoanut, pineapple and many other kinds of delicious fruit grow. High up on the hill in the rear of the town are to be seen the Government house, barracks, hospital, the signal station and a fine church.

At ten o'clock we went ashore. The first place we visited was the market-house. This was quite a large building, taking up over half a block. Fruits, vegetables and different articles were displayed for sale. There were also stalls filled with tinware, hardware, etc.

Many of the natives speak the English language well. I was delighted to meet with some who talked to me about our blessed Jesus.

Close by the market-house stands the Episcopal church, a fine building.

A WEDDING IN AFRICA,

A large gathering of people stood around the gates of the Episcopal church and were kept back by the police. We had been informed that a grand wedding would take place in this church at 11 o'clock. The daughter of a Free Town merchant was to be married to a merchant from Switzerland. We went to the gate and were at once admitted. A large company had assembled, among whom could be seen all colors, from black to white. Nearly all of them were fashionably dressed.

Soon the bride and groom made their appearance, with their relatives and many friends. Mr. Broadhurst, the bride's father, is a wealthy merchant, and very popular among all classes in Free Town. On this occasion all the principal business houses in the town were closed. After the marriage we took a walk along the street leading from the church to the residence of the bride. Along the entire way flags were hanging out of almost every window. In many places ropes were stretched across the street with flags and mottoes. We were invited by the bride's father to his house. The bride had many valu-

able presents.   A handsome silver set was sent
to her from England.

The most pleasing feature in Free Town, and
from what I hear in the colony also, is the great
progress made by the messengers of peace.
Nothing has or can civilize and elevate like the
word of God.   Christian schools have long since
been established, and for years have made most
wonderful progress.

There is hardly a trading post on the west
coast that has not some business man, clerk or
native missionary educated at Sierra Leone.
High schools have been established for the
training of native teachers and preachers.   The
advancement of the people is indeed astonishing.
There, too, are native merchants doing a large
business with some of the wealthiest firms in
London.

LIBERIA.

Our next stopping-place was Grand Bassa. We had to anchor three miles out, so we could not see much of the town. I was much disappointed that we did not stop at Monrovia, but on my return to England I had the opportunity to do so. The scenery along the coast of Liberia from Grand Cape Mount to the Gulf of Guinea, a distance of about 600 miles, is indeed grand. A few miles from the coast the country rises to hills, with gigantic trees, presenting a panorama that can only be described by a skillful artist.

Monrovia is the capitol of the Republic. It rests on a beautiful hill overlooking the sea, surrounded by trees. There are many very fine buildings in the city, which are creditable to the Monrovian people. The President's house is built of brick, as are also many others of the buildings. Many are built of stone. The wharves face the sea, where there are colored firms doing a large business with England, Scotland, Germany and America.

While in Monrovia for a short time I called, in company with Hon. John H. Smith, U. S. Consul, to see Mr. Sherman, who does a large business, both with England and America. After my return to England I wrote to Mr. Sherman for information regarding the articles of trade. This is the answer: "The articles of trade are palm oil, palm kernels, coffee, ivory, camwood, ginger and rubber. Many of our merchants do a business of $100,000 to $150,000 a year. One of Messrs. Gates & Porterfield's vessels left here for New York on the 7th inst., (April 7th, 1880) with a cargo of $50,000 worth, collected within two months. In this cargo were 118,000 pounds of coffee.

The soil of Liberia is extremely fertile, and will produce all kinds of tropical fruits and produce, sugar-cane, indigo, Indian corn, rice, cotton, cocoa, peanuts and coffee, the finest in the world. Vegetables are cultivated with great success. There are to be found the finest dye-woods, the ebony, the gum plant and the gigantic palm trees which produce the palm oil. On my way to England from Africa 1,500 casks were shipped on the same steamer to Liverpool, a good share of it being shipped from the coast of Liberia. Goats, swine, sheep, cattle and fowls all thrive in Liberia.

This republic has a glorious work to accomplish in the future. She will undoubtedly be in time the most prosperous State on the west coast of Africa. With the civil, social and religious advantages she enjoys, she must succeed. The annexation of the kingdom of Medina, with

FIVE HUNDRED THOUSAND INHABITANTS,

and her wide and fertile domains extending over two hundred miles into the interior, will no doubt inspire renewed energy in giving fuller opportunities for the advancement of the gospel, as well as an open door for civilization and commerce.

Above all, thank God! the truth is having "free course," and being "glorified" in the republic. Much zeal and perseverance have been displayed throughout the republic. Fine churches, school buildings and a nice college, are to be seen in Monrovia. Oh! see how many doors are being opened in Africa for Christian workers, who will go and tell the lost about our blessed Jesus!

November 30, at 6 o'clock in the morning, we arrived at Nifou on the coast of Liberia. I counted forty-nine canoes with two or three men in each, going out fishing. At twenty-five minutes to ten we stopped at Grand Cess, Liberia. Here fifteen canoes came out, with from three to twenty men in each, some with cloth around their waists, others with nothing on. I saw one man with a string around his waist and a large straw hat on.

These are the Kroo tribe, the Aborigines of a part of Liberia. They are a fine-looking people and very industrious. But for this class of people, I do not know what the European traders or the African Steamship Companies would do. All the steamers reaching Sierra Leone and the .coast of Liberia take on board a gang of "Kroo-men" to do the work of the ship in the hot climate. One hundred and thirty were taken on board to go down the coast to work. Many of them speak the broken English well.

It is quite a sight to see these people coming out to meet the steamer in their canoes. They are very light, carved out of one piece of wood, formed like a cigar. They are propelled by several of the men sitting down upon their heels in the bottom of the boat. Their yells as they approach the steamer are frightful when they come on board to work. Each man selects a name to suit himself, "Salt Water," "Coffee," "Shilling," "Glass Bottles," "Pea Soup," "Bottle of Beer," and the like, are common names among them. "Coffee" seems to be the most favorite. I wish I could say more about Liberia and its surroundings, but my space is limited.

WESTERN COAST TOWNS.

The more important towns on the west coast
are Elmina, quite an important town of 18,000
to 20,000 inhabitants, also Cape Coast Castle,
which is a beautiful place with its ports, light
house, signal station and large castle. Around
on the heights are to be seen beautiful houses of
the wealthy natives and Europeans. Accra is
another beautiful and important place. These
are all on the gold coast.

LAGOS

is said to be the most populous town on the west
coast. It has wide streets, nice stores and many
fine dwellings. They have their markets, sol-
diers, police force, churches, schools, court
house, custom house, Government house and
barracks. The population is estimated to be
about 50,000.

BONNY,

one of our stopping places, was in past years a
favorite rendezvous for slave ships. It has only
been about 12 or 15 years since they were all
cannibals. It is said that even now in some
parts near Bonny the barbarous custom of burying twins immediately after their birth, pre-

vails. It is so unhealthy at this place that European merchants live in hulks out on the river.

Archdeacon Crowther, a native, who has charge of the mission work, invited me to dine with him,* Princess Florance Siscelia Peble Pepper being present. Here I had the great pleasure of

DINING WITH AN AFRICAN PRINCESS.

She and her brother, King George, were both educated in England. Mr. Crowther took me to the school, where I was delighted to hear the children repeat passages of scripture, give their opinions about them, tell who wrote them, then go through history, arithmetic and geography, all of which they were well acquainted with.

I took a walk around among the native huts. I saw several huts having skulls hung up in them. I was told, by Mr. Crowther, that these were the skulls of captives taken in battle, that these people, years ago were cannibals, and had eaten the flesh of their enemies to make them brave. Thank God, through the influence of mission work and the spread of the gospel among these people, this custom has passed away, and the people are ashamed to be told that they once ate the flesh of their fellow-men. Not only has the preaching of the gospel done great good in Bonny, but far into the interior they are giving up their idols, and bowing to the "one true God."

---

*At some of these places we stop three or four days.

ASHANTEE AND DAHOMEY.

In traveling on the west coast of Africa you often hear of Ashantee and Dahomey, two very powerful kingdoms. The Ashantees are said to be the most numerous, warlike and powerful. This kingdom lies inland from the English settlements, between the rivers Assini and Volta, and has been estimated to have a population of four million people, and are noted for their skill in manufacturing cotton, earthenware and swords.

GOLD IS FOUND IN GREAT ABUNDANCE

in this country. Information given by Bowdich, Dupuis and others, show how these gentlemen were struck with the display of gold years ago. They found the attendants of the King laden with with ornaments of gold. The common articles for daily use were made of gold. But, oh ! how repulsive to read of the barbarous customs of

OFFERING HUMAN SACRIFICES.

These gentlemen saw at the King's palace the royal executioner, with his hatchet on his breast and the fatal blood-stained stool before him, ready, at the sound of the death drum, to do his fearful work. They heard that the King had recently murdered, over his mother's grave, three hundred victims. On the death of a royal person many hundred people are massacred. In late years, through the influence of missionaries and the authorities at Cape-Coast Castle, there has not been so much of this wholesale slaughtering of human lives, yet many are often murdered.

DAHOMEY

is another powerful kingdom in West Africa, separated from Ashantee by the river Volta. The wholesale murder in years past, was one of the chief features in their religious and state ceremonies. Abomey, the capitol of Dahomey, has been for many years the human slaughterhouse, where the King, chiefs and people have found their greatest pleasure and excitement in sacrificing as many (it has been estimated) as 2000 human victims at one grand custom. These people not only murder a large number of people on the death of a great man, but believe that in the other world a King is still a King, a slave is still a slave ; hence they kill annually so many slaves to send to the departed King. Also, whenever the King wants to send a message to his deceased relatives he delivers it to one of his slaves, whose head is instantly cut off, that he may carry the message to the other world, that the deceased may know that they are not forgotten. A few years ago when the King of Dahomey died, 280 of his wives were murdered.

Thank God, through the influence of Christian civilization, this is not so bad now as in past years. The King's palace at Abomey is said to be surrounded by a clay wall twenty feet high, the top of which is covered with human skulls.

AT OUR DESTINATION.

After stopping a short time at the island of Fernando Po, where we were entertained by the wife of the British Consul, we arrived at Victoria, Cameroons, on the afternoon of Saturday, December 14, 1878. This was our destination. Victoria is a beautiful little town of 500 inhabitants fronting Ambas Bay, with a commanding view of both bay and sea. On the north, south and east are high hills. In the distance can be seen the Cameroons Mountains, 13,000 feet above the level of the sea. The town is beautifully laid out with broad streets. Each house has a large yard and garden, in many of which are to be seen the palm, lime, cocoanut, breadfruit, custard-fruit, orange, banana and plantain trees. The cottages are neat and clean, built after the style of European cottages. These are occupied by the English-speaking people who are native Christians, and many of them have, for long years, been earnest workers for our blessed Jesus.

The next day after our arrival being Sabbath, Rev. R. W. Thomson, missionary in charge, invited me to take the morning service. A few minutes to 7 o'clock the bell rang, we were soon at the church, a fine stone building capable of seating 350 to 400 people. In a short time quite a number of well-dressed, intelligent-looking people had assembled. I gave out a hymn and they sang as well as many congregations I have preached to in America and England. When I commenced to read, nearly all of them opened their bibles to follow me in the lesson. Here I had the opportunity for the first time in my life, to speak for my blessed Jesus in Africa, the land of my fathers. I took for my text : " Believe on the Lord Jesus Christ, and thou shalt be saved." Acts, 16 : 31. I cannot remember of preaching to a more attentive audience.

At 10 o'clock we all went to ·the Sabbath school. Rev. C. H. Richardson and myself were invited to take classes ; my class was of young men. All of them

COULD READ THE BIBLE.

At the close of the school I requested the children to sing "Come to the Savior." They sang it beautifully. The school was well attended and perfect order was observed during the services.

For years Victoria has been a city of refuge. The late Rev. Alfred Saker, who labored in Africa about 30 years, established this station in the year 1858. He purchased from the natives (for the Baptist Missionary Society of Great Britain) a tract of land extending ten miles along the coast and five miles inland. Victoria is about the center. Here no natives are allowed to hold slaves or sell their daughters for wives, as is the custom. Here no one is allowed to be punished for witchcraft, etc. Each man is allowed to have as many wives as he is able to purchase among the natives. On my return to the coast from the interior I stopped with a chief who had forty wives.

At Victoria no man is allowed to have more than one wife. It often happens among the natives that when a child dies one wife will accuse another of having witched it. The woman is at once arrested and made to drink the juice of a wood called cass wood, which often kills them at once. Men also are often accused of witchcraft and are compelled to drink this juice. If they die they are guilty. If they recover (as some do who have strong constitutions) they are made to pay. If these people who are condemned can make their escape to Victoria they are safe.

The missionaries and christians have for years rescued many of these people who were on the very eve of being put to death. In one month I think that Rev. Q. W. Thomson rescued eight from the hands of these people, who had been condemned to death. To-day there are over 400 of these refugees in Victoria, where they are brought under the influence of the gospel and their children taught in the day school. Many of them have become christians.

For years there has been another repulsive custom. When a mother dies and there are no relatives to take the infants or young children, they are

PUT INTO THE GRAVE WITH THEIR MOTHER.

I am sorry I cannot now remember how many children Mrs. Alfred Saker (who was a mother among the Cameroas people for years) rescued and brought up in her own house. Many of them lived to be men and women. Some became teachers, and two or three are now in active service for the Master. Had it not been for the messengers of peace who went with undaunted courage and unceasing faith, these men and women condemned for witchcraft would have been lost.

Dear friend, you who now read these pages, you who were born in this christian land where you have the gospel, my prayer is that if you cannot go to Africa to preach the gospel or teach the people, you will at once resolve to do all you can to send others to teach and preach. While we are in this christian land enjoying gospel privileges, millions are slaves to superstition and witchcraft in Africa, perishing for want of the word of life.

> "Shall we whose souls are lighted
>   By wisdom from on high,
> Shall we to men benighted,
>   The light of life deny?
> God forbid.   Give a thought to Africa."

THE INTERIOR.

We had not been in Victoria three days before I was taken with the fever. January 20th Rev. C. H. Richardson and Rev. Q. W. Thomas left for the interior, to select a new station ; I being ill, could not go. On the 4th of February Mr. Thomas returned. Mr. Richardson having suffered with fever had been left at Bakundu, 80 miles in the interior, with two native Christians. Bakundu had been selected as the new mission station, hence he would remain there until joined by his wife, Mrs. Johnson and myself. The only roads through this country are narrow foot paths from town to town, sometimes in the tracks of the elephant. All provisions or luggage must be carried on men's heads. The account we had of the route was anything but favorable to Mrs. Johnson and Mrs. Richardson,—high hills to climb, large streams to cross. Although we knew that the traders along the river objected to interior mission work, we concluded we would go by water on account of the ladies. Mr. Greenfell, a merchant, volunteered to go with us.

On Thursday, the 6th of February, before day in the morning (after a sweet season of prayer with Rev. Mr. Thomson and the native brethren) we left Victoria in an open row-boat propelled by four Kroo men, followed by a large canoe with our provisions and eight men. At night we came to Mungo Creek. Here our interpreter and guide lost his way. We had intended to get by Mungo and Mbungo, the two principal towns, in the night. We passed Mungo, but at daybreak we found ourselves between the two towns. About 8 o'clock we got under the bank of the river, took out our things and prepared breakfast under the palm trees.

About one o'clock we found we had been discovered by the natives, and we accordingly left in the afternoon. As we passed Mbungo there were a few people at the beach, to whom we spoke, and passed unmolested. On Friday night a man passed us in a canoe, and commenced to beat his drum as he went on up the river. These people can

TALK TO EACH OTHER ON THEIR DRUMS

almost as well as we send a message in this country by telegraph. They have schools to teach their children this art. On this occasion this man said on his drum, "White man come to take our country." The natives with me (12 in number) did not tell me of this until the next day. Saturday morning at nine o'clock several canoes passed us, as we were taking our breakfast on the river, with from 15 to 20 men in each. Seeing they were well armed with guns and cutlasses, I began to feel suspicious. Soon we were off. About ten o'clock we came up to them. They had all stopped on the beach, put on their war caps and stood in line along the river.

We were ordered to come ashore. We told them we would not ; if they had anything to say come out in their canoes. They tried to make us leave our boat and go on the beach, but we resolved to stay in our boat. I do not know of any hour in my life when I realized the promise of my blessed Jesus more than in this hour, "Lo, I am with you alway." I said to my wife and her sister, Mrs. Richardson, we leaned upon the Lord.

At one time we were surrounded by nearly a hundred men armed with their cutlasses, ready to cut into us as soon as the young Prince would give command. We soon found that it was impossible for us to proceed. Hence

WE HAD TO RETURN AS PRISONERS

to Mungo. We were in six hours of Bakundu beach. Late in the night we arrived at Mungo. Here they wanted us to leave our boat and go into the town and see the King. We knew how superstitious they were about our English boat, so we resolved if we had to die, to die in this boat.

There were many of the traders at Mungo who

could talk English, and who knew how the English protected the missionaries. Mr. Greenfel, who had been several years in Africa and knew something of the people, threatened them with English authority. After the king and his men held a consultation, he said to me: "You must pay for passing through my country." To this we agreed. I gave him a large overcoat, a bag of rice, a box of sugar, a blanket and a barrel of crackers. While he was admiring the coat (which he had put on) we shoved off.

We arrived in Victoria on Sunday afternoon, having been three nights and four days on the water in this open row-boat. In one week from our return to Victoria we commenced our journey overland. Mrs. Richardson and Mrs. Johnson were carried in hammocks when they did not prefer to walk. Our provisions and luggage were carried on men's heads.

I have already mentioned that the best roads in this part of Africa are mere foot-paths through the forest, from town to town, on which the natives walk single file a few yards from each other, each man with his load on his head and his cutlass in his hand, or at his side, to defend himself against any beast or serpent that may be in the path. This was the way we started out of Victoria when we commenced our long journey of 80 miles through the wilderness. As we advanced into the interior we found the people along the route in a condition we had least expected to see. They had their fixed dwellings, many of them built neatly of bamboo, well thatched with mats made from the palm fronds. They had their

GARDENS AND FARMS, THEIR LAWS AND CUSTOMS,

so that wherever we stopped at night we and our goods were safe.

There are some eight or ten towns between Victoria and Bakundu. We left Victoria on Monday morning. On the following Saturday afternoon we arrived at Bakundu, where we found Mr. Richardson well. We had a company of 30 men with us when we arrived. It created much excitement.

The first thing I was most struck with was the joy of the old king. For years he had desired to have a missionary in his town to teach the people, as he had heard the natives were taught on the coast. Not only the king, but his sons and all his head men seemed delighted at our arrival. On Sunday we held a meeting in an old, unoccupied house. We found the people to be slaves to superstition and witchcraft, but not so bad as the other tribes around them.

The custom of giving cass wood juice prevailed here as among the Bakwilli people, of whom I have made mention. The first case we heard of was a young man in the town who was accused of witching his sister's child. He was made very ill from the effects of the juice, but finally recovered. As soon as we heard of it, Mr. Richardson, who was always fearless and ready on all occasions to admonish the people, went at once to the king and told him how wrong it was to allow such a practice. The king promised to put a stop to it. He kept his word. During the nine months I was in the interior I did not hear of another such case.

When we first arrived at Bakundu we could hardly sleep at night, for the yells of the people in their dance and the beating of their drums. This was kept up day and night. They knew nothing of the Sabbath. Hence they continued their drum beating Sundays as on other days. Mr. Richardson went to the king to have a law passed that no work or drum beating or dancing should be done on the Sabbath. The old man at once agreed to do so. The people then wanted to know how they could tell when Sunday came. Mr. Richardson had a trumpet which he would (walk up and down the street every Friday night) blow, telling the people that the next day was Saturday, that they must bring enough provisions from their farms to last over Sunday.

THEY HAD GREAT FAITH IN WHAT THE BIBLE SAID.

On one occasion while Mr. Richardson was away with men at Victoria, the women came to me to get me to ask the Bible if their husbands were safe.

A DYING KING.

Soon after our arrived in Bakundu we all commenced to pray that God would convert the King. Soon the old man was taken sick; he sent for us; we attended him; gave him medicine which seemed to do him good; but we soon found that he could not recover. I think he must have been about 90 years old. One day he sent for me and I found him very ill. He had a wooden bowl sitting by his bed in which was a liquid thick and black: this he was taking once in a while as I talked with him. I asked him what it was. He said: "Witch make me sick, tell me not to take white man's medicine, and I take this medicine, get my stomach full, old witch come in my mouth, go in my stomach, he get blind and come out." I tried to persuade him to believe that all power was in the hands of God, that by believing and trusting Him all these fears would leave him. He had always listened attentively to what we had to tell him about the great plan of salvation.

We continued to visit him, and day after day he would send for medicine. One Sabbath afternoon my wife and I both lay ill in bed. Mr. and

Mrs. Richardson went into the town to hold
service; our house was outside of the gate of the
town.   He found the king was very ill.   The excitement was such that he could not hold the
meeting, so he returned home.   We were soon sent
for.   I was hardly able to get out of bed, but we
were soon in his presence.   The house was full of
men.   Women were not allowed to see him, not
even his wives.   One man sat at his back to hold
him up, and two men on each side, three of them
his sons.   As soon as we entered the room they
gave us stools to sit on.   The old man was very
weak, and looking as if he would soon pass from
time into eternity, looked first at Mr. Richardson
and then at me.   His youngest son "Ngatee,"
about ten years old, was called to his side.   He
took one hand of the lad's and put it into Mr.
Richardson's hand, the other into mine and said,
"I give this boy to you.   Take him and bring him
up as your own child; dress him like white man;
teach him to talk English and to read and write;
His brothers will get a wife for him."   He requested that we should also take the girl whom
they selected and keep her in the family and ed-
ucate her. He then said, "Don't fear; I'm going
now.

THE TOWN BELONGS TO ME, AND I NOW GIVE IT TO YOU.
My son Etau will succeed me.   Take care of him;
be a father to him and the people."   This son
Etau was about 30 years old.   He then requested

Mr. Richardson to take the names of all the boys
in the royal family and head men, and com-
mence school at once. Some 60 names were taken
the next day. Mr. Richardson then told again
the story of God's great love, that if he would
believe and trust in the word of God we would
meet him in heaven. At this there came a groan
and nodding of the heads of the sons and several
present, as if to say yes, or amen! I then said
"Ta Ta Nambulee," (for that was what he was
called) "you say you are going now, are you prepared to meet God?" "Ah!" said the old man,
"I have been ill these ten days, and he has taken
care of me; I can still trust him." We then
wanted to pray with him, but his sons requested
that we should let him rest as he was so weak.
We left our interpreter to hear what he could after
we had gone. After we had gone he said to his
son who was to succeed him, "Etau, whatever
these men tell you, believe it, I have found them
to be true men. I have seen God. See all
those people there, (pointing to the wall of his
mud house) they have come after me; they are
a rejoicing people."

Oh how we all rejoiced to hear this, so often
we had prayed for the conversion of this man.
One evening we sent our cook up to tell his experience to the old man, and also to pray with him.
He was a native convert. The old man enjoyed
it very much, and said: "Tell white man (they

all called us white) to pray to God and ask Him, if it is His will, please spare me a little longer. If not, please prepare me to meet Him."

For years this old man had heard of the work of the missionaries on the coast, 80 miles away. A year before we settled at Bakundu, Rev. Q. W. Thomson had visited him and promised to send a missionary to labor among his people. After we had settled among them he was anxious to see how we would succeed. He sent for the women, who do nearly all the work on the farms, and charged them not to work on the Sabbath, as it was God's day; that they must attend divine service on that day. He was taken to his farm, where he died in two or three days. We arrived in Bakundu Feb. 22d, 1879. The king died in the latter part of June. Here was a heathen who had only met the missionaries twice as they passed through his town. Then after hearing us about four months, he dies, as I really believe, a convert to christianity. And yet there are thousands in this christian land who never give this all-important matter a prayerful consideration. Oh what gratitude we ought to feel that we have been favored with the gospel.

I believe there are to-day in west Africa thousands like Ta Ta Nambulee who have heard through traders and travelers something about the great mission work and the one true God, who are anxious to hear more, who are not sat-

isfied in their condition, who want to know, but
have no way to know, their souls craving something to rest upon, something stronger, better
and firmer than idols of wood and stone. In
this condition they toil on from year to year like
the beas in the cage, ever walking up and down,
trying to escape, but never able to succeed.
How can they hear without a preacher?

> Come o'er and help us, is their cry,
> Come now, oh do not pass us by.
> We are seeking truth, we are seeking light,
> We seek deliverance from dark night.
> Can you who have the gospel fail
> To hear our cry, our doleful wail?

I believe God is now preparing the hearts of
the people to receive the truth. Let us send it
to them.

The attention the people gave to the preached
word Sabbath after Sabbath was very encourag-
ing. The men and boys always attend in the
morning, the women in the afternoon. One Sabbath afternoon it was found that some of the women had gone to their farms to work. The
young king at once left the meeting, called a
meeting of his brothers and the head men, passed
a law that "if any man or woman worked on
the Sabbath they should pay a cow. If they
had no cow their house should be pulled down
over their heads."

In Bakundu, as in all the towns along the
route,

THE CHILDREN ARE ALL NAKED.

Men and women have a cloth around their waists. The men generally dress more than the women. As soon as they became more acquainted with us they wanted us to give them clothing. Tobacco and cloth is the only currency used in the interior.

Some of the people on the Mungo river raise corn and sweet potatoes. The staple food of the country is plantain. This you can stew, bake, fry or roast. It is a very good substitute for bread. The yam and cocoa are plentiful, the latter very much like potatoes when cooked. These they raise on their farms. They have fowls, goats, sheep and cattle all through the country. The sheep have hair like goats. The Bakundu people are not a savage people, or not as cruel as their neighbors and other tribes. You never hear of any murdering among them as you do among other tribes. They are very kind-hearted, and in every way differ much from the surrounding and coast tribes. Many of the west African tribes are continually at war. You hear of their

DRINKING THE BLOOD AND EATING THE HEARTS

of their enemies ; of walls covered with human skulls ; of a pavement made of human skulls, to walk on ; of human sacrifice. To this we have already referred. Truly, "The dark places of the earth are full of the habitations of cruelty."

Some tribes pay homage to lakes, rivers and mountains, believing that their gods live there. In some places large houses are kept for serpents. To these miserable reptiles they pay homage. At Dix Cove, on the west coast, it is said they have a crocodile which they worship. At Duketown, on the old Calabar river, in 1859 human flesh was sold at market as we sell beef in our markets here at home. I saw nothing of this at Bakundu.

These people have queer superstitions, and one must be among them to realize what slaves they are to them. When it rains they beat their drums to make it stop. There is a bird which makes a noise at night something like an owl. This is called a witch bird. When it is heard the children are afraid to go out, and guns are fired to frighten it away. In passing their farms you often see a stick stuck into the ground, split at the top, with a piece of cloth or wood put crosswise in it. I was told that this was to keep off thieves. One night a man came to me to get medicine for his child, and soon after he left the house he cried out in the most pitiful manner, "Witch come to take my child."

During the rainy season food generally becomes scarce, the elephants destroy the plantain farms, and the continual heavy rains keep them from hunting. One day I heard the natives shouting and singing near our house while it

was raining very hard. I looked out and saw a
crowd of men at the gate putting up palm
branches over the gate, and burying something
under the gateway. I was told that the palm
branches were to keep away famine, and that
what was buried was to draw game near the
town. It was indeed remarkable to see the
earnestness and the excitement of these people
while they were going through this performance.
After seing us light a match, the news was soon
spread through the country that we could carry
fire in our pockets, and take it out and make it
burn when we wanted to. One day, some ten
or twelve men and boys came to see us light a
match. When I took the box out of my pocket,
they ran as though I had taken out a pistol to
shoot them. "That's it, that's it," cried the
knowing ones, and their consternation seemed
to have no bounds.

These people have their Ju Ju Houses or
Fetish Temples like the rest of the tribes; there
are three in Bakundu. Here they have their
secret meetings. What they do, and how, I
could never find out, but this I do know, that
the preaching of the gospel and the untiring zeal
of Mr. Richardson, fighting against error, has
been the means of many of the young men
losing faith in Ju Ju. Before I left Bakundu,
Mr. Richardson had commenced to hold divine
services in the Ju Ju Temples.

THEY BELIEVE IN A SUPREME BEING.

They believe that there is a great being who has great power, but make no connection between Him and themselves, neither expect anything from Him; neither do they attribute to Him any qualities, good or bad. Their gods were many. The name of their general profession is "Ekodde;" when they are performing some custom they will tell you they are "doing Ekodde." Certain medicines have certain names, and certain powers attributed to them. They will take a certain medicine and use it, then ask the Ekodde God, or power governing that medicine, to give it power. They have a wooden man in their Ju Ju temple called "Mosango," upon which they take oath, believing that any person who puts his hand on the head of this image, who has told a lie or done wrong, will be exposed.

I was told by a native Christian that men often hold out until they get to the Ju Ju house, but so great is their fear of "Mosango" that they will confess before putting their hand on his head. They used to think that after death they would roam about in some unseen form, often troubling those who possessed the property they left behind.

Rev. Mr. Wilson, a native missionary, told me that the lives of many of the Bakwille people were miserable all the time, nothing but one continual dread of the witch, what he can and may do at any time. I believe it to be the same to a great extent among the Bakundu people.

But, thank God, the everlasting gospel is gradually making a great change in the people, even in this short time.

I was greatly impressed with the great

ANXIETY OF THE PEOPLE TO BE TAUGHT.

One of their chief desires seemed to be, while I was there, to see their children taught how to read and write and to talk the English language. Mr. Richardson had not commenced the school more than two days before he had over a hundred boys. The men, among them and the young king, wanted me to teach them while Mr. Richardson taught the children.

I was much moved one Sabbath morning while Mr. Richardson was telling about the love of our blessed Jesus, a man asked if their children could tell them the same story out of the Bible, when he had taught them to read and talk English.

> "They love to hear the old, old story
> Of Jesus and His love."

One Sabbath evening after service some 15 or 20 came to our house to be more fully informed about the plan of salvation, and this, too, with out having been invited to come. It is remark able to see how fast the children learn. But it will take many years to get them out of their superstitions.

WHAT THEY EAT.

In reference to their food we may say they eat everything, from a snake to an elephant. Dogs are quite a delicacy among them. One of the king's sons brought in a serpent one day. I think it must have been 16 feet long. They had quite a feast over it. Monkey is another favorite meat. They are great hunters; sometimes they have wonderful tales to tell about the monkeys and baboons.

The Bakundu people are very clever. They make their own fishing and hunting nets, and baskets and beautiful bags out of grass. I have a few with me. We had not been in Bakundu long before we found they were anxious to have clothes, especially shirts. We would buy meat of them with shirts. Soon quite a number of them, especially the head men, had shirts. One Sabbath morning, just before service, a man came in with his shirt folded under his arm. Just as service was about to begin, he put it on.

It was, indeed, extraordinary to me to see the attention these people gave when telling them the good news. A woman came to Mr. Richardson one day, and said: "I have never stopped praying since you first told us what the Bible said." This was several months after his talk with her.

IN MEMORIAM.

About the first of March, 1879, my dear, faithful, good, loving, christian wife (after nursing me until I got better,) was taken down with the fever. We hardly thought she would live ; but she got better. From that time until her death, she was never well. About six weeks before her death, she became so much better that we all thought she would soon be well ; but she insisted that she would not live long.

During the months of May and June, we were building our new house. I would often say how much better we would be in the new house, and what we would do. She would say: "Yes ; that's if I live to see it." After the rainy season set in, I said we must be careful about our provisions (we had to send to England for our provisions), as it will be a long time before we can get any more. "Yes," said my dear wife ; " but I am going to enjoy these that are here.

I WILL NOT BE HERE LONG."

Her Bible was her daily study. Mr. Spurgeon's sermons, which were sent out monthly, by Mr. Wigney, from London, she would read and reread. Day after day, from morning till night, and from week to week, she would find no greater comfort than reading her Bible.

On Sunday morning, June 29th, I lay in bed, ill. Mr. and Mrs. Richardson had gone to hold services in the town. She sat down near the bed and commenced to talk over our married life of fifteen years and seven months. The following Friday, July the 4th, she was taken down with the fever. The following Monday she slept nearly all day. At night she said: "All of this day has been lost; I have not read my Bible any." I read for her.

Monday night she was delirious nearly all night. Soon in the morning she said: "Although my mind leaves me at times, I have not lost sight of that rest, that rest!" He that the Son makes free shall be free indeed. Her favorite text was (and she often repeated it):

"I shall be satisfied when I awake with thy likeness."— Psalm 17 : 15.

About noon she lost her speech. In this state she lay until 8 o'clock Wednesday evening, July 9th, when

MY BLESSED JESUS CALLED HER HOME

from the land of our fathers to "that rest," there to be crowned. The house was soon filled with the natives, who showed great sympathy. Late in the night Mr. Richardson told them they could go home (king, queen and head men were all present). They said: "No. This is a bereavement in which we are all concerned. It is our grief as well as yours." Thus they remained all night. Though she could not speak but a few words of the language, she was indeed dearly beloved by the men, women and children of Bakundu. They all called her "mamma."

RETURNING HOME.

From the time I arrived at Bakundu to the death of my wife, I had never been well; from this time I commenced to get worse. In November Rev. Mr. Wilson, native missionary, came up from the coast to accompany me to Victoria. I was so ill and weak that I had to be carried 80 miles in a hammock by the natives.

Soon I returned to England, where medical men advised my return to America, on account of my health. Rev. C. H. Richardson was appointed by the Baptist Missionary Society of Great Britain to take my place, where he is now laboring successfully. He has long since been without an interpreter, and

PREACHES TO THE PEOPLE IN THEIR OWN LANGUAGE.

He and his dear wife are 80 miles into the interior, with no assistance of native Christians from the coast. While he is laboring at this new station, there are also many of God's messengers at new stations on the West Coast and in Central Africa, who need our prayers and help. Pray for them. A great work is going on in that benighted land. We in this land of light must do all we can to send more help.

A few years ago the great interior was closed to the Christian world and enveloped in mystery. But, thank God, the great work of explorers has opened a door to the interior. Mr. Stanley, in following up the great work commenced by Dr. Livingstone, has pointed out to the Christian world that vast tract of land lying between the West Coast and the Lake Mountains—a district of 860,000 square miles.

"Once above the falls," says Mr. Stanley, "We have the half of Africa before us, with one vast populous plain teeming with life and thickly inhabited. In fact, I know of no place in Africa, after Ugogo, so thickly populated." Thank God, since these discoveries a great work has commenced in Central Africa, and the name of my blessed Jesus is being published among thousands who for years have sat in darkness.

Stations have been opened and are working with great success at Lake Nyassa, Ujiji, Uganda, San Salvador, and on the Great Congo or Living Stone River. And yet we hear the cry: "Come over and help us." Millions are yet without the Gospel. The last words of our blessed Jesus were: "Go ye into all the world and preach the Gospel to every creature. He that believeth and is baptized shall be saved; but he that believeth not shall be damned."— Mark 16:15-16. "Whosoever shall call upon the name of the Lord shall be saved."—Rom. 10:13. In the great commission our blessed Jesus says he that believeth and is baptized shall be saved. Paul says, Rom. 10:14: "How shall they believe in Him of whom they have not heard? And how shall they hear without a preacher?" Oh, my dear friend, "Give a thought to Africa." It has indeed been well said that Africa is the most profoundly interesting of missionary lands, because it is God's greatest providential mystery. Great in its antiquity, great in its colossal wickedness, great in its hideous wrongs, great in its tremendous difficulties as a mission field, great in its costly missionary sacrifices, great in its future possibilities for Christ and the world." Let us undertake great things for Africa, with all of our hearts and souls, and we shall have a great blessing.

"AFRICA FOR JESUS."

Africa for Jesus
   Is the burden of my song ;
But methinks it draweth near,
   And shall not tarry long.

Africa for Jesus,
   For nothing else will do ;
No other power can save
   From their wretchedness and woe.

Africa for Jesus,
   Shout the words along,
Till the christians everywhere,
   Echo the gladsome song.

Africa for Jesus,
   Till they work with might and main,
To win fresh victories for His cross,
   New trophies for Him gain.

Africa for Jesus,
   Till all her chiefs shall own
The right of Him o'er them to reign,
   Who sits on heaven's throne.

Africa for Jesus,
   Till each battle ax and spear
Be of the past, no more to make
   Each other dread and fear.

Africa for Jesus,
   That her cannibal sons, too,
May be taught to see the wickedness
   Of the dreadful things they do.

Africa for Jesus,
   For Satan doth oppose,
And in that land he raiseth
   Many, many foes.

Africa for Jesus.
   Yes, he shall surely win,
He is the Lord, the conqueror
   O'er every woe and sin.

Written for Thomas L. Johnson, by Mrs. E. Shrewsbury, Northampton, England.